THIS BOOK IS A GIFT
OF FRIENDS
OF THE ORINDA LIBRARY

JESSE
JAMES

LEGENDARY REBEL AND OUTLAW

SPECIAL LIVES IN HISTORY THAT BECOME

Signature LIVES

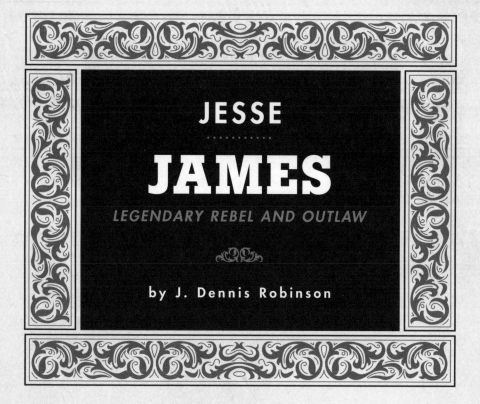

JESSE

JAMES

LEGENDARY REBEL AND OUTLAW

by J. Dennis Robinson

Content Advisers: Chip DeMann, John J. Koblas,
Earl Weinmann, and Mark Fagerwick, Executive
Director, Northfield Historical Society,
Northfield, Minnesota

Reading Adviser: Susan Kesselring, M.A.,
Literacy Educator, Rosemount–Apple Valley–
Eagan (Minnesota) School District

COMPASS POINT BOOKS ✦ MINNEAPOLIS, MINNESOTA

Compass Point Books
3109 West 50th Street, #115
Minneapolis, MN 55410

Visit Compass Point Books on the Internet at *www.compasspointbooks.com*
or e-mail your request to *custserv@compasspointbooks.com*

Editor: Jennifer VanVoorst
Page Production: Blue Tricycle
Photo Researchers: Marcie C. Spence and Svetlana Zhurkin
Cartographer: XNR Productions, Inc.
Library Consultant: Kathleen Baxter

Art Director: Jaime Martens
Creative Director: Keith Griffin
Editorial Director: Carol Jones
Managing Editor: Catherine Neitge

Library of Congress Cataloging-in-Publication Data
Robinson, J. Dennis.
    Jesse James : legendary rebel and outlaw / by J. Dennis Robinson.
        p. cm.—(Signature lives)
    Includes bibliographical references and index.
    ISBN-13: 978-0-7565-1871-4 (hardcover)
    ISBN-10: 0-7565-1871-7 (hardcover)
    ISBN-13: 978-0-7565-2104-2 (paperback)
    ISBN-10: 0-7565-2104-1 (paperback)
    1. James, Jesse, 1847–1882—Juvenile literature. 2. Outlaws—West
(U.S.)—Biography—Juvenile literature. 3. Frontier and pioneer life—West
(U.S.)—Juvenile literature. 4. West (U.S.)—History—1860–1890—
Juvenile literature. 5. West (U.S.)—Biography—Juvenile literature.
I. Title. II. Series.
    F594.J27R63 2007
    364.15'52092—dc22   2006002997

AMERICAN FRONTIER ERA

The young United States was growing at a rapid pace. Settlers were pushing west, conquering and building from coast to coast. World leaders hammered out historic agreements, such as the Louisiana Purchase in 1803, which drastically increased U.S. territory. This westward movement often led to bitter conflicts with Native Americans trying to protect their way of life and their traditional lands. Life on the frontier was often filled with danger and difficulties. The people who wove their way into American history overcame these challenges with a courage and conviction that defined an era and shaped a nation.

Table of Contents

1

MAN
AND MYTH

✦

Jesse James was running out of steam. By 1881, the bearded outlaw who leaped aboard the train in a small depot outside Kansas City, Missouri, was tired of being hunted and shot and feared. The wild blue-eyed young rebel who had fought so fiercely for the Confederate cause during the Civil War was now a married man with a wife and two small children. Many of the outlaws he had ridden with were dead or in jail, and Jesse James had begun telling close family members that he, too, wanted to quit his life of crime.

But thieves and murderers, Jesse knew, could never retire. In 15 years, he, his brother Frank, and their outlaw gang had robbed as many as 20 banks, trains, and stagecoaches. They had killed at least 10 innocent men since the end of the Civil War in 1865 and

Jesse James and his gang robbed trains and banks throughout the Midwest in the years following the Civil War.

had stolen perhaps $150,000, worth nearly $3 million today. They had narrowly escaped every law enforcement officer, volunteer posse, and private detective who had pursued them.

By the summer of 1881, as his new gang boarded a Chicago Rock Island and Pacific Railroad train, Jesse James was the best-known criminal in the United States. He and Frank were the subject of popular books and of magazine and newspaper articles. Much of what had been written about them was pure fiction. Authors who had never met the James brothers turned their often-brutal crimes into romantic and exciting tales about the Wild West.

According to these adventure stories, Jesse James never harmed an innocent man. He refused to steal from Southerners, poor farmers, or women. He was not a bad man, some said, but a heroic figure fighting against a corrupt government and greedy banks and railroad companies. Polite, witty, and well-mannered, their make-believe Jesse James robbed the rich and gave to the poor. The stories were popular, and one of their biggest

Jesse James is usually grouped with outlaws of the Wild West, but he lived most of his life just west of the Mississippi River. Most of his crimes took place in the center of the United States, not far from his home base near present-day Kearney, Missouri. Because of frequent robberies in the northwestern Missouri area bordering Kansas, Iowa, and Nebraska, this region became known as "bandit country."

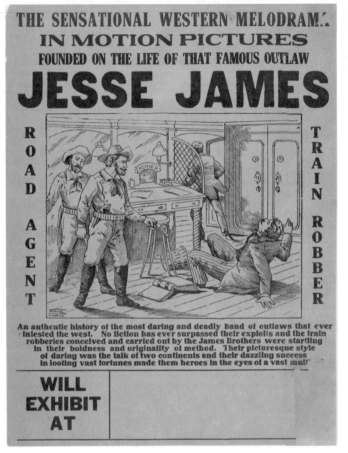

fans was Jesse James himself. Jesse craved fame and loved attention.

But the facts tell a very different story. There is no evidence, for example, that Jesse James ever gave any money to the poor. Much of it he gambled away or spent while hiding and moving his family from place to place. He usually robbed men and women, rich and poor, Northerner and Southerner equally.

His crimes were often poorly planned, and his gang members were often harsh, threatening, and even drunk. When challenged or angry, he killed without a second thought. Jesse and Frank James shared an amazing ability to elude the law, but they often escaped being killed or captured by pure good luck.

But the James brothers had plenty of bad luck, too. The July 15, 1881, Chicago Rock Island and Pacific Railroad robbery, for example, was originally planned for June. Jesse's cousin Wood Hite and friend Dick Liddil were going to join the attack, but a torrential rain washed away their escape route. Days later, while setting up another robbery, Jesse was overtaken by a terrible toothache and rushed to Kansas City to find a dentist.

On July 14, the outlaws heard that a lot of cash was coming by railroad express, but they all missed the train carrying the money. The following evening, however, Jesse James' gang finally pulled off the train robbery. In the dark of night, three of the bandits smashed a window and entered the train as it whistled through Daviess County just outside Winston, roughly 65 miles (104 kilometers) from Kansas City.

William Westfall, the conductor, was moving through the smoking car collecting tickets. He was near the rear of the car when the robbers shouted, "Hands up!" Before the conductor had time to respond, Jesse shot him in the back, moved closer, and then shot him again. As Westfall's body fell onto the rear platform, Jesse James and another robber or two began firing wildly, killing a bystander named Frank McMillan.

The passengers on the train erupted in a panic as the robbers moved to the train's express car. The outlaws forced the engineer to stop the train and then broke into the car. After U.S. Express Company agent Charles Murray opened the safe, the robbers

Jesse James and his gang often used violence in carrying out their robberies.

knocked him unconscious with a blow to the head from a gun. Then they vanished into the dark surrounding woods.

Dividing the loot, the gang members discovered they had picked the wrong train again. The take from the robbery was just $126 per man at the cost of two innocent lives. Historians have suggested that the James boys may have known William Westfall and killed him out of revenge. Or perhaps they thought the conductor was carrying a gun. Either way, they committed murder. And judging from the angry reaction of the newspapers, most Missouri citizens were fed up with the violent crime spree of the James gang. This was not the daring hero described in the exciting "dime novels," but the real flesh-and-blood Jesse James.

The public outcry prompted Missouri Governor Thomas Crittenden to take strong action against Jesse James and his gang. Crittenden convinced the railroad company to offer a reward of $10,000 each for the capture and conviction of Jesse and Frank James, and $5,000 apiece for each of the other gang members. Despite the

> *Publishers were eager to take advantage of the growing fame of the James brothers and their outlaw gang. Short, inexpensively produced books known as nickel or dime novels, provided fictionalized accounts of the real events reported in the newspapers. The Train Robbers: Or, A Story of the James Boys, was published in June 1881, and was the first of many dime novels to advance the James gang legend.*

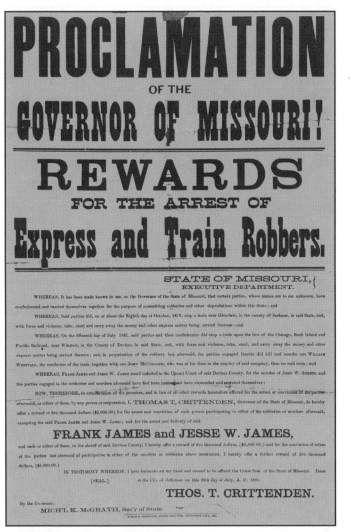

Posters publicized the Missouri governor's reward for the capture and conviction of Frank and Jesse James.

risk, Jesse James struck another train on September 7, 1881. It was to be his last. This time the gang blocked the tracks at a slow bend in the road near Independence, Missouri, known as Blue Cut. The leader of the gang, a masked man with a full dark beard, announced that he was the infamous Jesse James. Again, the haul was small. This time, the gang harassed and robbed the passengers, including Southerners, poor farmers, and women.

Among the robbers at Blue Cut was a young man named Charlie Ford, whose brother Bob wanted to join the gang. But secretly, the Ford brothers were more attracted to the governor's $10,000 reward than the meager income to be made robbing train passengers. Bob wanted to be as famous as Jesse James. Seven months later, Bob Ford shot Jesse James in the back of the head. But with a single

A song titled "The Ballad of Jesse James" fueled Jesse's fame even after his death.

BUT THAT DIRTY LITTLE COWARD, THAT SHOT MR. HOWARD, HAS LAID POOR JESSE IN HIS GRAVE
AMERICAN FOLKSONG ENG. BY JOHN HELD JR. WITH A HI AND A HO

bullet, Bob Ford made Jesse James more famous than ever and branded himself a traitor and a coward.

Ford murdered an outlaw, but the imaginary Jesse James lived on. Many would believe he was a boy driven to crime by forces he could not control. This heroic figure would show up endlessly in popular books, Hollywood movies, television shows, and even video games. But the real Jesse James was a very different man. ◌

Jesse James (1847–1882)

2 THE GOOD SONS

 broc

Jesse James, one of the most wanted men in American history, was the son of a well-educated Baptist minister. While attending college in Kentucky, his father, Robert James, met 16-year-old Zerelda Cole. The couple married in December 1841 and, after Robert's graduation, moved to Clay County, Missouri, to live with Zerelda's mother. Zerelda had inherited some money, and the young couple used it to purchase 275 acres (110 hectares) of land outside what is now the town of Kearney. There, they began raising tobacco and hemp, a woody plant used to manufacture canvas and rope.

By all accounts, Robert James was a dynamic and popular preacher. During his ministry, the congregation of the New Hope Baptist

Republican candidate Abraham Lincoln debated his opponent, Democrat Stephen Douglas, in the 1858 Senate race. They disagreed on slavery and would later compete for the presidency.

Church increased from 20 members to 280. He also raised money to help found William Jewell College, a Baptist institution, in the nearby county seat of Liberty. Eldest son Alexander Franklin James was born on January 10, 1843, when Zerelda was not quite 18 years old. Called Frank, the eldest James son was serious and bookish. Frank usually carried a Bible and was later known to quote from Shakespeare while robbing his victims.

After a second son died in infancy, Zerelda gave birth to Jesse Woodson James. Born on September 5, 1847, Jesse took after his mother. Both were tall with steel-blue eyes and had long oval faces, and wild personalities. A daughter, Susan Lavinia, arrived in 1849. Many years later, a newspaper reported that Zerelda's passionate attention to her children could "be likened to nothing else but a tigress's love for her cubs."

For a short time, the James farm thrived. It was a great place to grow up—for the three white children, at

When Missouri applied to enter the Union in 1818, there was an equal number of free and slave states. Because slavery was legal in Missouri, it was expected to become a slave state. The following year, Maine applied to the Union as a free state. The Missouri Compromise of 1820 was created to maintain the balance of power. It said that all new territories above the southern border of Missouri (except Missouri itself) would be free states, and the territory below that line would be slave states. This compromise lasted until 1854, when the Kansas-Nebraska Act allowed slavery in formerly free territories.

least. For the family's seven black slaves, however, it was a prison. Almost every business in the region had at least one enslaved African-American hand or servant as they were called, who worked the farm, cooked the meals, and provided skilled labor. Like many of their neighbors, Zerelda and Robert James believed in slavery, and there is evidence that the man known as Preacher James bought and sold

In the 1800s, African-American slave labor formed the backbone of farming operations throughout the South.

black children. At this time, the family property included 30 sheep, six head of cattle, three horses, a pair of oxen, and seven human beings. There was one adult slave, known as Aunt Charlotte, and six children. The children, who ranged in age from 2 to 11, were named Nancy, Alexander, Maria, Mason, and Hannah. The name of the sixth child is unknown. Jesse James was very likely nursed by a black nanny and played daily among these children.

Shortly after Jesse's birth, rumors of gold discovered in California reached Missouri, and over the next few years, many men from Clay County ventured West in search of riches. In the spring of 1850, Robert James told members of the New Hope Baptist Church that he would be leaving to preach the gospel to this new wave of fortune hunters. Though some members of his congregation approved of his missionary work, others doubted his motives and counted him among the fortune hunters. Later reports speculated that he left home to escape the controlling influence of his wife, who was known

The greatest gold rush in U.S. history began on January 24, 1848, when a gold nugget was discovered at the Sutter's Mill sawmill near Coloma, California. News of the discovery quickly spread, and by 1849, a large-scale gold rush was under way. Within a year, the California city of San Francisco grew from 1,000 residents to nearly 25,000 as people arrived from all over the world in search of riches. By 1850, California had enough people to be admitted to the Union as the 31st state.

for being sharp-tongued and domineering. Whatever his reason, Robert left his wife and three young children and headed west. Three-year-old Jesse reportedly held his father's leg and begged him not to go.

Robert wrote to his family as he traveled. In an April letter, Robert signed off by asking Zerelda to "kiss Jesse for me and tell Franklin to be a good boy and learn fast." This letter was one of his last. Soon after he arrived in California, he died of fever at a gold rush outpost known as Hangtown.

The Reverend Robert James (1818–1850)

Robert's death changed everything. Although she was strong-willed and intelligent, his widow, Zerelda, was in trouble. Her money had paid for the farm, but by law, as a woman, she could not inherit her husband's property since Robert had left no will. Instead, the farm was held in guardianship by family friends, the Wests. With three children and seven slaves to feed and clothe, Zerelda found herself deeply in debt. Forced to auction off one of her slaves and many of her possessions, Jesse's mother was reduced to accepting charity from relatives and the local church.

In 1852, apparently to improve her dire financial situation, Zerelda married Benjamin Simms, a wealthy Clay County farmer. Simms was twice her age and not interested in the three young children Zerelda brought to the marriage. At his insistence, Jesse, Frank, and Susan were sent to live with the Wests. But Zerelda feared that if she did not take her children back, "they would never more recognize her, so she separated from Mr. Simms." Zerelda moved in with the Wests, and a divorce seemed likely when Simms unexpectedly died. According to one report, he fell from his horse.

In 1855, soon after Jesse's 8th birthday, Zerelda married again. With this marriage, her third husband, Dr. Reuben Samuel, became the legal guardian of the James children. He also assumed guardianship of the James farm, where the family now lived. At the time, farming was a much more respectable profession than medicine, and Samuel traded in his medical practice to work the farm with his stepsons and slaves. Samuel was reportedly "an easy, good natured, good for nothing fellow ... completely under the control of his wife." This third marriage lasted, many believe, because the easygoing Samuel did not challenge his wife or try to tell Frank and Jesse what to do. The boys, in turn, liked their new stepfather. Zerelda and

The James farm, photographed in 1877, was Jesse's home base for much of his life.

Samuel eventually had four children of their own—Sarah, John, Fannie, and Archie.

Frank and Jesse attended a local school and received at least an elementary education. But history offers few clues to life in the Samuel household. Early stories about the James boys sometimes depict Frank as a wild troublemaker and Jesse as the innocent younger brother. Others imply that Jesse was a cruel and angry child who was prone to violence. But there was violence all around at that time. The long-held national debate over slavery was about to explode into a long and bloody civil war. As the nation expanded westward, the legal debate raged

When the Civil War began, both the Union and the Confederacy sought the support of the border states. North Carolina, Tennessee, Arkansas, and Virginia joined with the South, but Virginians in the western part of the state were loyal to the Union and formed the new state of West Virginia in 1863. Delaware, Maryland, Kentucky, and Missouri stayed in the Union, but secessionist groups in Kentucky and Missouri set up separate state governments and sent representatives to the Confederate Congress. Some of the heaviest fighting of the war occurred in the border states.

in Washington, D.C.: Would new states allow or prohibit slavery? The heated argument was already splitting the country in half along the border states that separated North from South.

Missouri was one of these border states. The fighting had already begun in the nearby Kansas Territory, just over the border from where the James boys were growing up. According to the Kansas-Nebraska Act of 1854, new states entering the Union would decide for themselves whether to become slave states or free states. The result, both sides knew, could shift the delicate balance in government between North and South. Pro- and antislavery forces rushed to fill the Kansas region with people who supported their views. Vigilantes from each side took the law into their own hands and battled the other in a conflict that became known as Bleeding Kansas.

The idea that states could determine their own position on slavery was called popular sovereignty, a phrase the James boys certainly heard often in their

younger years. Stephen A. Douglas, a pro-slavery Democratic senator from Illinois, proposed the idea of popular sovereignty. In 1860, he and two other candidates ran for president against Abraham Lincoln, an Illinois Republican who opposed the spread of slavery. Not one man in Clay County, Missouri, voted for Lincoln, and his election was seen in the South as a call to war. As slaveholders, there was no question which side the Samuel family was on. Jesse and his older brother were ready to fight anyone who wanted to change their way of life. ✆

Disagreements between Kansas and Missouri residents over the issue of slavery led to violence, earning the conflict the name "Bleeding Kansas."

3 HORRORS OF WAR

Chapter

ϛ⌒⌒ϟ

Jesse James was only 13 years old when Abraham Lincoln became president of the United States. Shortly after Lincoln was elected in 1860, Southern states began leaving the Union. Eventually, 11 states joined together to form their own Confederate States of America with their own president, Jefferson Davis. When Union soldiers refused to surrender control of Fort Sumter in South Carolina, Confederate forces attacked on April 12, 1861. The Civil War had begun.

Three days after the attack on Fort Sumter, President Lincoln called for the states that did not secede to deliver 75,000 new Union soldiers in order to quickly crush the new Confederacy. Most Northerners saw the Confederates as traitors who wanted to destroy the U.S. government. But in Clay County,

Missouri painter George Caleb Bingham depicted Union soldiers ordering Missouri residents to leave their homes.

During the Civil War, border states such as Missouri eventually found themselves having to take sides.

Missouri, Mr. Lincoln's War, as it was called, was seen as an invasion by Union forces into a separate Southern country.

Although Missouri stayed in the Union, three-quarters of its residents sympathized with the Southern cause. Missouri Governor Claiborne F. Jackson

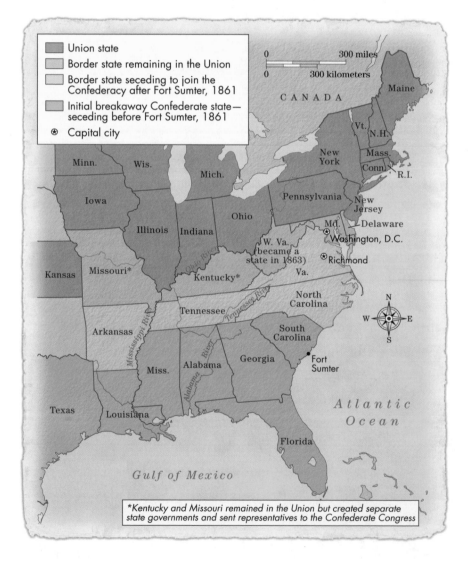

Union state
Border state remaining in the Union
Border state seceding to join the Confederacy after Fort Sumter, 1861
Initial breakaway Confederate state—seceding before Fort Sumter, 1861
⊛ Capital city

0   300 miles
0   300 kilometers

CANADA

Maine

Minn.   Wis.   Mich.

Vt.
N.H.

New York   Mass.
Conn.
R.I.

Iowa

Pennsylvania   New Jersey

Ohio

Md.   Delaware

Illinois   Indiana

⊛ Washington, D.C.

W. Va. became a state in 1863)   ⊛ Richmond

Kansas   Missouri*   Kentucky*   Va.

North Carolina

Tennessee

South Carolina

Arkansas

Miss.   Alabama   Georgia   Fort Sumter

Texas   Louisiana

Florida

Atlantic Ocean

N
W   E
S

Gulf of Mexico

*Kentucky and Missouri remained in the Union but created separate state governments and sent representatives to the Confederate Congress

refused to send men for what he called Lincoln's "unholy crusade." Instead, Jackson called for 50,000 men to join his own State Guard to keep the Union forces out of Missouri. Only 5,000 men answered his call. Among them was Jesse's big brother, 18-year-old Private Franklin James, who signed up with the Home Guard on May 4, 1861.

The attacks were fierce and bloody. Frank found himself fighting young Union soldiers from his own home state as well as abolitionists, called jayhawkers, who attacked from nearby Kansas. As the focus of the war moved to other states, the Missouri conflict turned into one small guerrilla band pitted against another for control of territory. Missouri citizens found themselves caught in the crossfire between rival gangs. Jayhawkers raided families who held slaves. Then Confederate guerrillas known as bushwhackers responded by attacking families that supported the Union cause. No one was safe.

Union forces captured Frank. When he took an oath promising not to fight on the side of the Confederates, he was released and sent home. But Frank soon broke his vow. This time he signed on

> *Over the next four years, the Civil War would claim 623,000 American lives—more than any other war in the nation's history. In fact, the Civil War is responsible for the deaths of nearly as many Americans as the combined American dead of all other wars from the Revolutionary War in America (1775–1783) through the Iraq War, which began in 2003.*

with William Clarke Quantrill, the leader of a savage band of guerrilla fighters.

With as few as a dozen men at a time, Quantrill's raiders ambushed Union soldiers and terrorized Union sympathizers. His band of irregulars did not fight like regular soldiers. They hid or disguised themselves, struck suddenly, inflicted as much damage as possible, and retreated quickly. Often they broke into even smaller groups, which made them harder to follow.

William Clarke Quantrill (1837–1865)

Catching these Missouri guerrillas was nearly impossible, since, unlike a regular army, they could melt into the towns and hillsides. To flush them out, the Union Army leaders made it illegal under penalty of death for Missouri civilians to help or hide the raiders. The Army could do this because it controlled the state government under martial law. The Army's 1863 order to Missouri citizens read in part:

All persons who shall knowingly harbor, conceal, aid, or abet, by furnishing food, clothing, information, protection, or any assistance whatever to any such emissary, Confederate officer or soldier, partisan ranger, bushwhacker, robber, or thief, shall be promptly executed.

Jesse James' stepfather was almost executed under this law. During the spring of 1863, a pro-Union militia stopped at the Samuels' place in Kearney looking for Frank, who had broken his oath of allegiance. Fifteen-year-old Jesse was plowing the field when he was grabbed by the throat and dragged back to the house. There, he saw troops tie Samuel's hands, place a rope around his neck, and throw the rope over a tree limb. They repeatedly hung and released Samuel until he told them that Frank was hiding nearby. Using the information gained by torturing Samuel, the troops discovered a band of Quantrill's men hiding in the woods playing poker. Five of these bushwhackers were reportedly killed, but Frank narrowly escaped, as he did time and again throughout his life.

On August 14, 1863, a warehouse in Kansas City holding Confederate political prisoners

William Clarke Quantrill led a bloodthirsty band of guerrillas who attacked Union soldiers and sympathizers. A former schoolteacher, he taught the James brothers the hit-and-run attack style that they used in their later robberies. Quantrill was a folk hero among some Southerners and was a popular subject with former Confederate writers during the years just after the Civil War.

Zerelda James was a fierce supporter of the Confederate cause. In fact, in 1863, Zerelda gave birth to a daughter whom she named Fannie Quantrell (a common spelling of the famous bushwhacker's name) "just to have a Quantrell in the family."

collapsed, killing five women and permanently crippling two others. In response, Quantrill and 450 raiders, including Frank James, brutally attacked the town of Lawrence, Kansas. In four hellish hours on August 21 they burned the place to the ground. Following Quantrill's orders to kill every male old enough to hold a gun, the bushwhackers murdered 200 men and boys. Four days later, the Union Army issued General Order Number 11, a military command that forced nearly all the citizens of the nearby Missouri counties to leave their homes. By driving most of the border population out of their houses, the Union Army leaders hoped to stop them from hiding and helping the guerrilla bands.

Quantrill's raiders did leave for a while and spent the winter in Texas. But Union soldiers went too far in forcing out the Missouri citizens. The soldiers robbed and torched a great many of the homes in the counties near the Kansas border that became known as the Burnt District. They killed not only guerrilla fighters and Confederate sympathizers but many innocent civilians as well.

In the space of a few short years, 16-year-old Jesse James' life had been turned upside down. He

had seen his stepfather tortured, his countryside destroyed, and his people oppressed. He had seen enough. He finally joined the bushwhackers in the spring of 1864 after they returned from Texas. Now reunited with Frank, it wasn't long before the pair fell under the command of William "Bloody Bill" Anderson, who had split from Quantrill's group to form a new band of guerrillas. Jesse admired

Quantrill and his raiders led an attack on Lawrence, Kansas, that ended with the city's destruction by fire.

Anderson's famous savagery and was eager to win his new leader's respect. Anderson, in turn, liked Jesse, whom he referred to as "the keenest and cleanest fighter in the command."

Jesse barely survived his early career as a bushwhacker. Soon after signing on, he was severely wounded while stealing a saddle from a local farmer. Spotting the teenage thief, the farmer stepped through the doorway of his house and shot Jesse in the chest. With brother Frank holding him in the saddle, Jesse was able to ride 4 miles (6.4 km) before he was placed in a stolen wagon. Jesse remembered, "They were driving fast and I was suffering so intensely that I wished every minute the soldiers would overtake and kill me."

His guerrilla companions ferried the wounded Jesse across the Missouri River and rushed him to an inn near Kansas City. The inn belonged to his uncle John Mimms. Jesse was hidden in an attic loft that could only be reached through a trapdoor inside a clothes closet. Here, near death, Jesse James met the woman he would one day marry. His first cousin Zee Mimms nursed the wounded boy back to health. Zee, short for Zerelda, was named after Jesse's mother, and these two women would remain loyal to him for life. Two months later, as soon as he was well enough to ride, Jesse James mounted his horse and rode back to join his rebel band. All that remained of this brush with death was a distinctive scar— a scar that would one day be used to identify James' body. ❧

Sixteen-year-old Jesse James was photographed during his first year as a bushwhacker.

4 FROM BATTLES TO BANKS

Chapter

ⲥⲟⲭⲟ

After recovering from his wounds, Jesse James rejoined Bloody Bill Anderson's guerrillas shortly before their most infamous raid. On September 27, 1864, roughly 80 of Anderson's rebels, most likely including Frank and Jesse James, attacked the tiny railroad village of Centralia, Missouri. The bushwhackers were always looking for ways to disrupt the flow of communications, soldiers, and supplies to the Union Army. While they waited for a train to arrive, they robbed a stagecoach, tore up the town's two stores, and got wildly drunk on stolen whiskey.

When a train finally approached the depot, Anderson's men forced it to stop by blocking the tracks. Twenty-five unarmed Union soldiers were on board, most of whom were heading home on leave from

Confederate General Robert E. Lee's surrender in 1865 to Union General Ulysses S. Grant (right) marked the near end of the Civil War and the beginning of a new career for Jesse James.

battle. The raiders marched the soldiers off the train, ordered them to strip off their uniforms, and shot them at close range. Only one soldier was allowed to live. After robbing the remaining civilian passengers, the guerrillas set fire to the empty train, which they sent speeding down the tracks. Then they burned the town.

William "Bloody Bill" Anderson (c. 1840–1864)

When a group of Union soldiers arrived in Centralia later in the afternoon, they found a few rebels remaining. The soldiers pursued them into the hills—and fell into a deadly trap. The rebels led the Union soldiers to a larger group that had gathered nearby to wait. This force ambushed and killed all 125 Union soldiers. Jesse James claimed responsibility for killing the commanding Union officer.

By the fall of 1864, the bloody Civil War had been raging for nearly four years. As the end of the war neared, the loosely run rebel groups began to fall apart. Bloody Bill Anderson was killed just weeks after the Centralia Massacre when he himself was ambushed by Union troops. To document his death,

someone tied Anderson's body in a chair and photographed him holding a pistol.

With the death of Bloody Bill, Jesse moved on to
a new group of raiders in Texas, and Frank went east
with William Quantrill, who reportedly was plotting
to kill President Lincoln. But Quantrill never got the
chance. On April 14, 1865, less than a week after General Robert E. Lee surrendered his Army of Northern
Virginia to Union General Ulysses S. Grant, a Southern sympathizer named John Wilkes Booth shot Abraham Lincoln. The president died the following day.

*President
Lincoln was
shot in plain
sight in a
crowded
theater.*

Before his death, Lincoln had offered a sweep-
ing pardon to Southern troops as part of the
surrender. Confederate soldiers and officers were

allowed to return home if they took an oath of loyalty to the Union. They were even allowed to keep their rifles. But Missouri's new leaders were unsure how to deal with the rebels who fought under men like Quantrill and Anderson. Did they too deserve to be pardoned? Guerrillas like the James brothers had not played by the rules and had never actually been members of the Confederate Army. They had worked outside the law, and the outlaws feared they would now be captured and imprisoned—

Confederate soldiers rolled up their flag after the end of the Civil War.

if not by the military, then possibly by local law enforcement officers.

Many bushwhackers surrendered to the Union Army and returned home to live normal lives. According to Jesse James, this is what he was doing on May 15, 1865, near Lexington, Missouri, when he was once again shot in the chest. In his story, he claimed he was carrying a white flag of surrender when a group of drunken Union soldiers shot his horse and then shot him. The soldiers likely thought Jesse was attacking or trying to evade capture when they fired on the teenager. The 36-caliber bullet pierced the right side of Jesse's chest, very close to the first wound.

He escaped on foot and later explained:

> *I was running through the woods pursued by two men on horseback ... and they were pressing me hard, every jump that I made, the blood would spurt out of my wound. ... [I]t seemed that my body was on fire.*

Everybody thought the wound would kill him, but Jesse cheated death a second time. He was discovered the next day by a farmer and taken to a local hotel. There, on May 21, he signed a loyalty oath like all surrendering Confederates and agreed to follow the laws of the United States.

After several weeks in Lexington, Jesse crossed the Missouri River and went to Kansas City, where he again spent time recovering at the home of his uncle John Mimms. Then, on July 15, he left for Rulo, Nebraska, to be cared for by his mother and stepfather. They had been living in Nebraska since being forced from their home in Kearney under General Order Number 11.

Gravely ill, Jesse hovered near death for months. Fearing his end was near, his mother claimed, Jesse asked to be taken back to Missouri so that he wouldn't die in a Northern state. But Jesse was too ill to travel with his family all the way to Kearney, so, after a steamboat trip down the Missouri River, he stopped again at the Mimms' home. Here, his cousin Zee once again nursed Jesse back to health, and the pair soon became secretly engaged.

Zerelda "Zee" Mimms (1845–1900)

Once he was well enough, Jesse James returned home to Kearney. There, he seemed to settle down to a quiet life on the family farm. His mother and stepfather had been allowed to return, and together they tried to pick up their shattered lives in Clay County. Frank surrendered and returned home from the East, and for a time, the James brothers seemed like decent, law-abiding citizens. Jesse even joined the local Baptist church. But this peaceful period was not all it appeared to be. Jesse and his brother had begun to meet with their fellow wartime raiders. They were bitter and restless, and their rebellion was unfinished. Though the Civil War had ended, the bushwhackers would find new ways to fight on. ✍

Jesse James carried the bullet from his 1865 shooting in his chest for the rest of his life. It was not recovered until 1995, when his body was exhumed for scientific study and the bullet was found in his grave.

5 BECOMING OUTLAWS

Chapter

❧⟋⟍⟋❧

On February 13, 1866, two men in long blue Union Army overcoats stepped into the Clay County Savings Bank in Liberty, Missouri. One of them asked bank cashier William Bird for change from a large bill. Suddenly the two men jumped over the counter and pointed their cocked guns at Bird and his father, the only two employees in the bank. One robber struck Bird with a pistol and forced him to collect the money in the vault while the other robber gathered the cash and government bonds into a cotton wheat sack along with some gold and silver. Bird's father was told to lock himself in the vault with his son. "He told me that if I did not go in instantly he would shoot me down. I went in," Bird's father later recalled.

The Birds quickly escaped from the vault, which

Frank James (center) wore a Confederate soldier's coat in an 1867 photograph with his brother Jesse (right) and guerrilla leader Fletch Taylor.

A 19th-century illustration shows the main room of a bank's safety vault.

they had not locked, and tried to raise an alarm, but it was too late. The robbers had escaped, taking more than $57,000 in bonds and currency with them. In addition to the two robbers, as many as 10 additional men were involved in the daytime robbery. Those stationed outside the bank quickly jumped on their horses, firing their guns in the air and shouting as they rode away. One of the bandits shot and killed a 19-year-old boy who just happened to be walking by. The young man was a student at William Jewell College, the school that years earlier Frank and Jesse James' father had helped found.

No one knows for sure who robbed the Liberty bank, but historians speculate that Frank and Jesse James may have been on the scene. Both brothers denied any involvement, as they did with every robbery that followed. Jesse claimed that he was still recovering from his wounds and was too ill for the rugged outlaw life. And according to family accounts, Jesse did travel to visit a doctor and then to bathe in the healing sulfur springs of Colorado. Some historians, however, suggest that Jesse's long, slow recovery was simply a smokescreen invented years later to cover up his early crimes. And every element of the Liberty bank robbery pointed to one conclusion: The bushwhackers were back.

It is easy to see how a few rebel bushwhackers became bandits. After all, in many ways the bushwhackers were outlaws during the Civil War, too. They were angry, aggressive young men fighting a common enemy on their home territory. As in modern street gangs, with no one else to trust, the members formed strong bonds that lasted for life. The war turned them into skilled riders and marksmen. They knew how to plan sudden attacks, frighten their victims, disguise their identities, and avoid capture. They bullied and killed without remorse.

Though the Civil War had ended, many bushwhackers still fought on in their hearts. The way Jesse James saw it, the Unionists had attacked his family, stolen his slaves, tortured his stepfather, shot him twice, and taken away his dignity. They left Clay County in shambles. There were few jobs, thanks in part to the new railroads that could import cheap labor and charge high rates to farmers transporting their goods. And the newly elected government of Missouri refused to allow former Confederates to run for office.

Back home in Clay County, 19-year-old Jesse grew bitter, bored, and discontented. Perhaps he turned to robbery as a way to get revenge on the powerful people who seemed to control his life. It likely seemed like easy money, as well, and it was certainly no more dangerous than the life he had known in wartime. Although Jesse repeatedly denied any involvement with robberies, money was coming from somewhere. He was described as being dressed up in expensive clothes and "quite dandified," according to one report. He wore a fancy new hat and rode a fine new horse.

Over the next two years, a number of holdups in Missouri towns followed a pattern similar to the bushwhacker bank job in Liberty. Four men took more than $2,000 from a Lexington bank and left when the teller refused to produce the key to the vault. Five gunmen wounded a banker in Savannah when he would not cooperate and then fled without a dime.

> *Most local citizens were angry with the bushwhackers and did not see them as heroes, as they are often depicted in movies today. When two suspected bandits were captured and jailed in St. Louis in 1868, a local mob dragged the prisoners to the edge of town and hanged them from the limb of a tree.*

In Richmond, robbers stole $4,000 and killed three townsmen during their escape. Thieves in Russellville, Kentucky, got away with an estimated $12,000. Many of the men suspected of the crimes had been members of William Quantrill's rebel band during the Civil War.

In 1869, a major robbery finally put the James brothers in the headlines and confirmed Jesse's role as a bank robber. On December 7 of that year, Jesse and Frank James entered the tiny Daviess County Savings Association in Gallatin, Missouri. Jesse approached the cashier and asked him to change a $100 bill. Suddenly, he thought he recognized the cashier as the man who had killed his former guerrilla leader,

A group of men gathered in front of a Gallatin building that once housed the bank robbed by Jesse and Frank James.

Bloody Bill Anderson. He shot the cashier—once in the chest and once in the head. The only other man in the bank, a lawyer, ran for the front door to alert the town as the bandits gathered up the money and fled. But they did not get away easily.

Alerted to the robbery, Gallatin citizens began shooting at the escaping robbers. Jesse's horse, spooked by gunfire, did not allow Jesse to mount. Jesse had gotten one foot in the stirrup when the horse bolted, dragging him helplessly down the street until he could untangle himself. In what has become a classic Hollywood moment, Frank James pulled his brother onto his own horse, and the two galloped away in a hail of bullets.

Jesse soon stole another horse from a nearby farmer as they rode toward Clay County, but his fine horse, left at the scene of the crime, was quickly identified as belonging to one of the James brothers. When the sheriff and a local posse reached the Samuel farm 50 miles (80 km) away in Kearney, Frank and Jesse burst from the barn on horseback, soared over the fence, and escaped.

The man Jesse had killed in the robbery, Captain John W. Sheets, was well-liked in Gallatin. He was both the cashier and the owner of the bank, and he had not killed Bloody Bill Anderson, as Jesse had suspected. It was a case of mistaken identity, the James family later claimed, but everyone else saw it as a case of cold-blooded murder. Jesse James—or someone using his name—wrote a letter to the *Kansas City Times* saying that he had not been in Gallatin at all. Still, the sheriff of Gallatin offered a $3,000 reward for the capture of Jesse and Frank James.

After the Gallatin robbery, the James brothers disappeared from view for more than a year. Adventure writers later filled in the missing time with their own wild stories. According to one legend, Frank

Over the course of his career as an outlaw, many rewards were offered for the capture of Jesse James.

and Jesse ran a trading post in Nebraska and had children with Native American wives. Historians, however, believe they drifted around Texas, Arkansas, Kentucky, and maybe even farther east.

The James brothers reappeared in Corydon, Iowa, on June 3, 1871. According to a popular legend, everyone in Corydon was gathered at a political rally outside of town when a man rode up and told them that the bank had just been robbed. Frank

The James gang's robberies centered on the brothers' home state of Missouri.

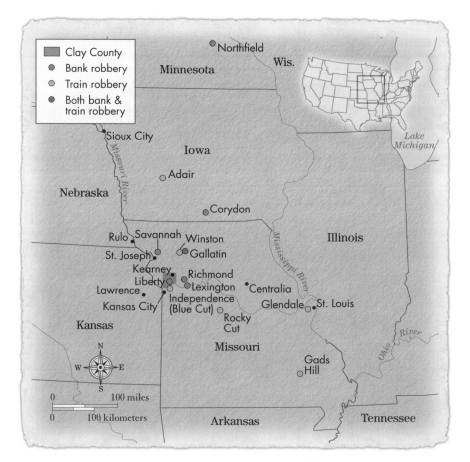

James, many believe, was the man who alerted the crowd as well as the man who robbed the bank. But again, Jesse James denied involvement. In another letter to the newspaper, he wrote of the claim of his involvement, "It is as base a falsehood as ever was uttered from human lips."

Though many historians today doubt their involvement, Jesse and Frank were next accused of robbing the Kansas City Fair on September 26, 1872. The thieves rode their horses through a large crowd to demand the cash taken in tickets to the fair. They got $978, a sizable sum, but just missed another $12,000 that had already been taken to the bank. When the ticket taker tried to hold onto the money, one of the robbers shot at him through the crowd. The bullet accidentally hit a young girl in the leg.

Glossing over the facts of the robbery, *The Kansas City Times* called the heist the "Most Dangerous and Daring Robbery of the Age." The author of the article, a former Confederate officer named John Newman Edwards, suggested that the bandits "deserve at least admiration for their bravery and their nerve." For Edwards, it was the beginning of a long and very successful effort to transform the James brothers from violent outlaws into great American action heroes.

Chapter

6 THE GREAT TRAIN ROBBERY

∽⌖∽

By 1873, Jesse James had attracted the attention of two men—one a loyal friend and one a bitter enemy—who were about to make him the most famous outlaw in the United States. The friend, John Newman Edwards, used his newspaper to defend Jesse and other Missouri bushwhackers. He mixed the truth with made-up stories, flowery language, and his own strong opinions to turn them into heroes. Two days after the Kansas City Fair robbery, he compared the bandits to King Arthur and the Knights of the Round Table and to Robin Hood and his Merry Men, both popular stories from England.

"What they did we condemn," Edwards wrote about the bandits soon after the robbery at the Kansas City Fair in 1872. "But the way they did it we cannot

Cows grazed near the site of an 1873 James gang robbery outside Adair, Iowa.

John Newman Edwards (1839–1889)

help admiring."

The local newspaper printed letters by Jesse James so often over the years that historians suspect that Edwards wrote them himself—or at least helped write them. It was Edwards who first told Missouri readers how law enforcement officials had tortured Jesse's stepfather by hanging him from his neck by a rope. He magnified Jesse's exploits in the Civil War and his failed attempt to surrender, depicting him not as an outlaw but as a victim. With no evidence at all, Edwards promoted the story that the James brothers gave some of their money to the poor. They never fired their guns, Edwards said, except in self-defense.

Edwards painted a romantic picture. The bandits were daring, resourceful, generous, kind, and polite to women, he said. Edwards reinvented James and his cohorts in the public mind, turning them from murderers and thieves into dashing gentlemen who just happened to be on the wrong side of the law. Many Missouri readers, broken by the war and crushed by the reconstruction that followed, saw a badly needed hero.

To Allan Pinkerton, founder of the Pinkerton National Detective Agency, nothing could be further from the truth. James caught Pinkerton's attention with the Corydon robbery, and it became for him a personal mission to capture Jesse James and other Missouri outlaws. Over the years, James and Pinkerton became bitter enemies. Both men were skilled at attracting a lot of publicity, and their rivalry made exciting reading in newspapers and cheap novels. The longer Pinkerton agents chased after James, the more famous James became.

"I consider Jesse James the worst man, without exception, in America," Pinkerton told a newspaper in 1879 after two of his agents were killed while track-ing the outlaws. "He is utterly devoid of fear, and has no more compunction about cold-blooded murder than he has about eat-ing his breakfast."

Then Jesse James tried something startling and, for

*Allan Pinkerton
(1819–1884)*

him, new. He began robbing trains. On July 21, 1873, a small gang of hooded bandits used a rope to pull the tracks out of line and stopped the Chicago Rock Island and Pacific Railroad outside Adair, Iowa. It was not a highly successful robbery and certainly not the work of gentlemen bandits. The train carried 3½ tons (3 metric tons) of gold and silver bullion, a king's ransom. But the outlaws were on horseback and unprepared to carry away the heavy treasure. After wrecking the train—killing the engineer in the process—and frightening the passengers, James and the other bandits had to leave most of the money behind. Openly angry and disappointed by their failure, they

Though Jesse James was probably the most famous outlaw of the time, other bandits robbed trains and banks across the country as well.

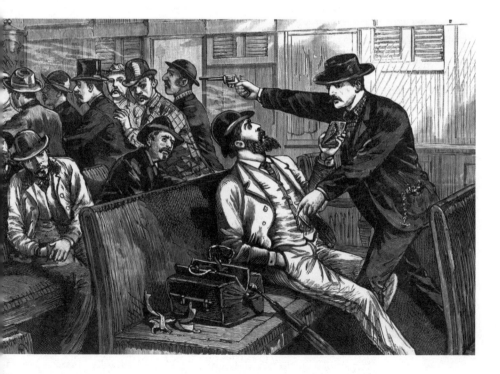

quickly escaped with less than $3,000 in loot.

Their next attempt on Saturday afternoon, January 31, 1874, showed better planning. The James gang, with Jesse now clearly in charge, struck the Iron Mountain Railroad at the little village of Gads Hill about 100 miles (160 km) south of St. Louis, Missouri. This time they robbed everyone from the passengers and the baggage clerk right down to the newsboy selling dime novels. No one was killed, but a few of the 25 passengers were punched and shoved around. The bandits joked as they stripped everyone of their valuables and quickly slipped away with more than $6,000. One gang member left behind a telegram, prepared in advance, giving details of the robbery to be printed in the newspaper.

True to form, editor Edwards blamed the robbery on the owners of the railroads, on Missouri government, on bankers, on the church, and even on the president of the United States—everyone except the James gang. These corrupt leaders, Edwards said, stole more every day than the bandits

Jesse James might not have been discovered by history without the constant positive newspaper coverage by John Newman Edwards. Born in Virginia, Edwards was a staunch Confederate who co-founded The Kansas City Times. He was so passionate about the Confederacy that he fought a duel over an argument in 1875. To rally support for the Confederate cause, Edwards created the sympathetic legend about Jesse James that survives today.

> *Founded in 1850 by Scottish immigrant Allan Pinkerton, the Pinkerton National Detective Agency was the nation's first security company. As a private police force, its employees tracked criminals like Butch Cassidy and the Sundance Kid. Allan Pinkerton, an abolitionist, coined the term "private eye" and used the slogan "We Never Sleep." The company still exists as Pinkerton's, Inc., which is owned by the Securitas Group.*

took from a robbery.

Railroad officials responded to the latest robbery by offering more reward money and hiring the Pinkerton agency to stop Jesse and his gang. But they failed. Six weeks later, Pinkerton agent Joseph Whicher was found dead with a bullet in his head on a road not far from the Samuel farm. The 26-year-old Whicher had tried to go undercover by applying for work as a hired hand at the farm of Reuben and Zerelda Samuel. This was a bad idea in a region where people were either loyal to the bushwhackers or afraid of them. Someone—many suspected the local sheriff—probably warned the James brothers, who then murdered the agent.

Missouri was becoming known as a breeding ground for criminals. People in Missouri did not appreciate the violence or the bad publicity, and politicians squabbled over who could best protect the state from dangerous men like Jesse James. Other critics blamed the people of Missouri themselves—especially Clay County citizens who protected and sheltered the outlaws in their homes.

Jesse James was becoming known around the world. As Missouri's reputation as the bandit state increased, so did the pressure on the Missouri government to do something about Jesse—and quickly. On January 25, 1875, the law struck back. In the middle of the night, Pinkerton agents tossed an explosive device through the window of the Samuel home in Kearney. It was intended to drive out Frank and Jesse, who were supposed to be hiding there. But the attack backfired when Reuben Samuel kicked the burning ball into the stove, and the stove exploded. Jesse's 9-year-old half brother Archie was killed by flying metal. His mother, Zerelda, was wounded and had to have her right arm removed. But Jesse and Frank, if they were even there at all, escaped once again. ❧

Zerelda James Samuel (1825–1911)

Chapter
7 FAMILY MAN

❧⟨✕⟩❧

The tragedy at the Samuel farm shifted public opinion in favor of the bandits. John Newman Edwards called the Pinkerton agents "midnight cowards and assassins." For Edwards, this was just more evidence that the detectives, the corporations, and the U.S. government had joined forces to crush the Southern way of life. Edwards and other romantic writers turned Jesse James and his men into a powerful symbol: the last rebels of the fallen Confederacy.

The true story, however, was much more complicated. Jesse was a killer and a thief, but he was also now a family man. On April 24, 1874, after a secret nine-year engagement, he married his cousin Zee Mimms. But it was not a normal life. The couple used false names and moved continually. Zee lived in constant fear that her husband would be killed or arrested.

Even the marriage ceremony was interrupted when detectives showed up in hopes of capturing James. Zee was forced to hide between layers of a feather bed while James jumped on his horse and tricked the agents into chasing him. After losing the detectives, he doubled back to Zee's sister's farm and rejoined the wedding.

Jesse's wife, Zee, stood by her husband and always claimed he was not as bad as others claimed him to be.

About the time James was settling down, the Pinkerton agency was accused of criminal behavior. A grand jury investigation in St. Louis found the detectives negligent in the attack in Kearney that maimed Jesse's mother and killed his half brother Archie. But no trial was ever held, and no one involved was ever punished. Opinion was now so heavily in favor of the outlaws that the Missouri state government almost gave the brothers amnesty for all their crimes. Amnesty meant they could be forgiven and not punished or thrown in jail. The proposed amnesty bill said the James boys were "too brave to be mean." But the bill was defeated in the legislature in March 1875.

In truth, Frank and Jesse were neither brave nor nice. The next month, they went to the home of their neighbor Daniel Askew in Kearney and accused him of being a spy for the Pinkertons. When Askew denied it, Frank shot him three times in the head. The James brothers then threatened other neighbors, ordering them to blame Askew's murder on the Pinkertons. People began to feel as frightened as they had during the Civil War. "If this killing business is not put a stop to," one newspaper reported, "our country will be ruined."

For a year after the murder, Clay County was quiet. Jesse and Zee moved to Nashville, Tennessee, where Zee gave birth to their son, also named Jesse. In this large city, James was able to blend into the crowd. He posed as a wheat speculator and went by the name John Davis Howard. Eventually, they traveled farther east, probably living with Frank and his wife, Annie, in Baltimore, Maryland.

In 1876, Frank and Jesse attended a large 100th anniversary celebration of the founding of the nation at Philadelphia, mixing freely with the crowds. No one recognized them. In fact, no one out-

Shortly after Jesse and Zee's wedding, Frank James got married, too. In June 1874, he eloped with a college graduate named Annie Ralston from Omaha. She did not tell her parents she had married the notorious Frank James. Loyal to the bitter end, Annie outlived all of them. She stayed at the James farm in Kearney until her death in 1944—and never gave a single interview.

side Clay County—not even the Pinkertons—knew exactly what the James boys looked like.

One physical description of Jesse came from the pen of Edwards, who pictured the outlaw almost as if he were a saint:

> *Jesse James ... has a face as smooth and innocent as the face of a school girl. The blue eyes, very clear and penetrating, are never at rest. His form is tall, graceful and capable of great endurance. ... Looking at his small white hands, with their long tapering fingers, one would not imagine that with a revolver they were among the quickest and deadliest hands in all the west.*

Jesse's hands, however, had a distinguishing feature that could confirm his identity. At age 16, while handling a gun in front of a group of Civil War bushwhackers, Jesse had accidentally shot off the tip of the index finger of his left hand. Instead of cursing when the pistol went off, Jesse shouted, "Dingus!" a slang word meaning stupid. From that point on, Dingus was the name his brother Frank called him.

Hiding out in the East under false names, posing most likely as cattle traders, the James brothers had one more chance to go straight and fade into history. In fact, not even Jesse's son knew who he really was. But Jesse was prone to gambling and racing fast horses. Whether he ran out of money, craved

fame, missed his home state, or
was addicted to danger is
unknown. Whatever his
motivation, early in the
summer of 1876, Jesse
James and his brother
Frank left their wives
in the East and headed
home to Missouri.

On July 6, 1876, the
James brothers hit the
Missouri Pacific Railway
at Rocky Cut, Missouri. Very
likely, Jesse had been reading
about himself in books by Edwards and

*Frank James
(1843–1915)*

others, and this time the gang behaved like dapper
highwaymen. Although they brandished pistols, the
masked bandits did not rob the frightened passengers
or harm anyone. They joked, acted politely, and disappeared with more than $15,000 in stolen money.

The Rocky Cut robbery was a great performance.
It featured Jesse James acting much as Edwards
imagined him. But it was not typical of the outlaw's
often-deadly appearances. His next caper, a bloody
raid on the First National Bank in distant Northfield,
Minnesota, was very nearly his last. ✎

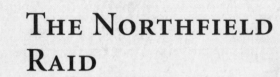

Chapter
8 THE NORTHFIELD RAID

༄༺✦༻༄

Even for a seasoned outlaw like Jesse James, the Northfield bank raid was a risky move. Jesse knew that carrying out a robbery so far from his home turf was full of hazards, but gang member Bill Stiles had convinced him that Minnesota banks were prime targets for robbery. According to Stiles, northern banks "held more money than they knew what to do with," and local residents would be completely taken by surprise. So in August 1876, Stiles, Jesse and Frank James, and five other outlaws ventured north to Minnesota to explore their options.

The men traveled in two separate groups to avoid attracting attention. But these Missouri bandits were fish out of water in the little Minnesota milling town 370 miles (592 km) north of their Missouri home.

Photographs show a victim of the Northfield raid, six gang members, and two men involved in their apprehension. The names of two of the dead outlaws, Clell Miller and Bill Chadwell, were transposed in the 1876 photo.

Their new horses were too fancy and expensive to avoid notice. They walked too boldly, swaggering down the streets like dangerous and important characters. Most men in Minnesota did not carry guns, so to disguise their Smith and Wesson revolvers, the outlaws all wore long linen coats called dusters, designed to protect a rider's clothing from trail dust.

The bandits posed as horse dealers and railroad surveyors, but their act was not convincing. They asked too many questions and flashed large rolls of cash. Many suspected these men were not all they pretended to be, but no one guessed their true motives. It wasn't until outlaws Charlie Pitts, Bob Younger, and Frank James entered Northfield's First National Bank at 2 P.M. on September 7, 1876, that the townspeople learned the real reason for the men's visit.

Nothing went right for the bad guys in Northfield. One of the robbers, Cole Younger, later confessed that the gang had been drinking too much wine. To make things worse, the three bank employees boldly refused to open the safe, even when one robber threatened to blow their brains out and another said he would cut their throats with a knife. One clerk bravely tried to grab a gun from beneath the teller's window while another tried to trap the robbers inside the vault. The frustrated robbers searched for the money themselves, missing a drawer that contained $3,000 in cash. During the distraction in the cramped

office area, one bank employee rushed out through a back door. He managed to escape the building, but not before being shot in the shoulder by one of the bandits.

The interior of the First National Bank has been restored to its 1876 appearance.

The situation outside the bank was even more desperate. Northfield residents spotted the robbers' lookouts standing guard outside the bank, and they began shouting to alert others to the robbery. Following the pattern they had been using since their bushwhacker days, the outlaws mounted their horses and rode through town shooting into the air and yelling. Their goal was to terrorize people and clear the streets for their escape. One man was shot and killed when he remained in the street after being ordered to "get in."

But the citizens of Northfield fought back. Men with rifles began firing from behind the windows of the hotel across the street. Others gathered large stones and hurled them like missiles at the bandits. Clell Miller, one of the robbers, was shot in the face with tiny pellets by a farmer with a shotgun, but he continued with the gun battle. He was eventually

While bandits attempted to rob the bank (in the middle of the block), fighting took place outside on the street.

killed with a shot to the shoulder. Bill Stiles, alias Bill Chadwell, who was serving as a lookout, sat low on his horse with his arms wrapped around the animal's neck for cover, but a local citizen's careful aim brought him down instantly with a fatal shot to the heart.

Outlaw Cole Younger rode up to the door of the Northfield bank and shouted to the robbers inside, "The game is up! Better get out, boys. They're killing all our men." But before they ran, one of the robbers—probably Frank—turned to Joseph Lee Heywood, a bank clerk who refused to cooperate in the robbery, and shot him in the head.

Having killed two innocent men and lost two of their own, the six remaining bandits quickly left town. Brothers Cole, Bob, and Jim Younger were wounded during their escape. Hungry, exhausted, and hurting, they traveled for two weeks in a heavy downpour. Sometimes they rode on stolen horses, but often they were on foot. Traveling in unfamiliar territory, they were pursued by local citizens who eventually numbered more than 1,000.

The bandits did not expect the citizens of Northfield to fight back. But the townspeople, many immigrant farmers, were fiercely independent, proud of their town, and wanted to keep their money. Today, the First National Bank has been restored to look exactly as it did in 1876. Every year, Northfield residents celebrate The Defeat of Jesse James Days. They re-enact the robbery and honor the local heroes who saved the day and helped put an end to the violent James gang.

After two weeks, bandit Charlie Pitts and the Youngers were cornered by their pursuers. In the gunfight that followed, Pitts was killed, Jim Younger's jaw was shattered, and Bob Younger was shot through the lung. Cole Younger was shot 11 times. Still, the three Younger brothers survived. They went to trial and were convicted of robbery and murder. Each spent more than two decades in prison.

The James gang's failed robbery in Northfield, Minnesota, led to the deaths of three gang members and the capture of three.

Though six of their gang members had either been killed or captured, the James brothers got away again. Even though the robbery of the Northfield bank had been a disaster, the escape of Jesse and Frank fueled the James legend. Their escape, according to one Minnesota witness, was "without parallel in the history of crime."

Three weeks after the Northfield raid, the James boys were spotted near Sioux City, Iowa, when they robbed a man of his clothes. Then, for the next three years, as far as the world knew, they disappeared.

For Frank James, the failed raid was a lesson well learned. He returned to his wife, and the pair settled again in Nashville, where Frank worked on his farm and became a father. Jesse and Zee rented a house in nearby Humphreys County. There, Zee gave birth to twin boys in 1878, who soon died, and then in 1879 to a girl she named Mary. Posing as grain speculator John Davis Howard, Jesse was again able to blend into the local community. He grew a long beard. Frank joined the local Methodist church. The brothers kept a low profile, except when gambling and racing their horses, and even made friends with a local sheriff.

While Frank was happy to remain anonymous, Jesse grew restless. He was the most famous criminal in the nation, but he could not reveal his true identity—not even to his own children. The murderous gunfighter had to pretend to be cowardly and avoid arguments and fights in order to preserve his secret identity. He began to gamble more and drink heavily. Though he continued to maintain his new identity as a law-abiding citizen, Jesse secretly

The James brothers' escape after the Northfield raid led to more books about them—and more fame.

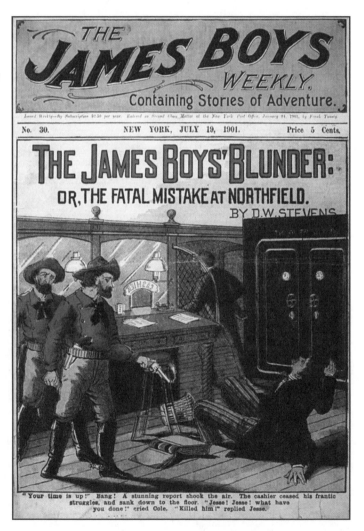

THE JAMES BOYS WEEKLY.

Containing Stories of Adventure.

Issued Weekly—By Subscription $2.50 per year. Entered as Second Class Matter at the New York Post Office, January 24, 1901, by Frank Tousey.

No. 30.   NEW YORK, JULY 19, 1901.   Price 5 Cents.

THE JAMES BOYS' BLUNDER:
OR, THE FATAL MISTAKE AT NORTHFIELD.
BY D.W. STEVENS

"Your time is up!" Bang! A stunning report shook the air. The cashier ceased his frantic struggles, and sank down to the floor. "Jesse! Jesse! what have you done!" cried Cole. "Killed him!" replied Jesse.

began to build a new gang and scout locations for new crimes.

On October 8, 1879, the new James gang, without brother Frank, hit the Chicago and Alton Railroad at the little Glendale depot east of Independence, Missouri. Following the pattern of earlier jobs, the six men robbed the local citizens, stopped the train, and emptied the express car. An agent who tried to save the money was hit in the face with a pistol. The bandits left a printed message for the newspapers and rode away firing their guns and shouting the Confederate rebel yell. They had expected to find $380,000 worth of gold and silver, but that train had gone down another track. The gang divided the $6,000 in cash and quickly separated. ᕙ

Chapter
9 DEATH OF
AN OUTLAW

❧⸙❧

The Glendale robbery put Jesse James back in the headlines, but the tide was turning against him. Missouri citizens were weary of lawlessness and saw the new James gang members as rude and greedy young toughs. People were horrified when the James gang killed two unarmed men over a mere $700 in a train robbery in Gallatin in 1881. A recent change in the state government meant that Jesse was no longer seen as a political rebel. Now he was just a middle-aged criminal, a rebel without a cause.

Jesse himself was tired of the outlaw life, but he could see no way out of it. He needed money to support his gambling habit and to keep his family hidden. With his family now in Missouri, he moved Zee, Mary, and young Jesse from town to town and house

Jesse James' death—shot in the back of the head by a fellow gang member—was a violent end to a violent life.

to house. They lived in a series of rented homes in Kansas City, sometimes staying as briefly as a single month before moving again. Neighbors soon grew suspicious of the secretive man they knew as Tom Howard, who had strange men coming and going from his house at all hours.

In November 1881, 34-year-old Jesse moved the family to a wood-frame house on Lafayette Street in St. Joseph, Missouri. Set among a grove of fruit trees at the top of a hill, the little house had a good view of anyone approaching. It was the outlaw's best and last hideout.

Zee James was photographed with children Jesse and Mary around the time of her husband's death.

Six-year-old Jesse Junior, who went by the name of Tim Howard, later wrote about his strange childhood. He remembered that his father was often missing for months at a time while a member of the gang stayed to protect his mother. Once there was a strange knock at the door. Instead of answering the knock, the man guarding the family simply fired his gun through the door. Jesse Junior grew up a lonely boy who fantasized about being able to settle down and make friends with other children. He wrote:

> My father always painted a bright future for me, of going to school, meeting other children, riding horses on a farm. I didn't know at the time that there was any reason why the future might not work out just that way.

In reality, however, the future for the James family was dark. The constant upheaval was taking a toll on Jesse James. More robberies were being blamed on him. More books about his adventures, real and imaginary, were being sold. His fame was putting money in the pockets of people he had never met. The reward for his capture was climbing, and the Pinkertons, he feared, were closing in. Jesse and Frank were angry at each other, but there was no one else they could trust.

As more gang members, both old and new, were hunted down and arrested, Jesse grew increasingly concerned about what the detectives might learn. Outlaw Bill Ryan, who knew the comings and goings

As a teenager, Jesse James Jr. got a job working for the son of Missouri Governor Thomas Crittenden, who also loaned him money. Jesse Junior ran a pawn shop and tobacco shop and earned money to go to law school. He was accused of robbing a train but was found not guilty. He married and had four children. Jesse Junior died in 1951. His sister Mary lived at the James farm with grandmother Zerelda, married a neighbor, and had three children. She died in 1935.

of the James gang, was sentenced to 25 years in jail. Jesse's cousin Clarence Hite was also captured and given 25 years. Jesse was so suspicious of Ed Miller, a young member of the new gang, that he shot him and secretly buried his body.

Then gang members Dick Liddil and Bob Ford got into an argument with Jesse's cousin Wood Hite and killed him. Liddil was so afraid of what Jesse would do to him if he found out that he turned himself in to the sheriff of Clay County in January 1882. Liddil made a deal: In exchange for his freedom, he offered evidence against the James brothers. Then Bob Ford met secretly with law enforcement officials and agreed to deliver Jesse James dead or alive.

Unaware of the plot against him, Jesse visited his mother at the farm in Kearney. Bob Ford and his brother Charlie went with him. According to legend, Zerelda Samuel warned her son to stay away from the sneaky Ford brothers. And Jesse may not have trusted them himself. "I am a little low-spirited," James reportedly told his mother as he left Kearney for the last time. "May be I'll never see you again."

Though he often claimed he wanted to retire from his life of crime, Jesse James never stopped being a robber. He was planning another job with Bob and Charlie Ford on April 3, 1882. On that day, Zee made breakfast for the three men. Just after 8 A.M., they moved into the living room of the little house in

Today, Jesse James' last home, in St. Joseph, Missouri, is open to visitors.

St. Joseph. Jesse brought along the morning newspaper. There was an article in the paper about the surrender of gang member Dick Liddil. The news upset Jesse. He had known Liddil since their bushwhacker days in the Civil War. They had both been part of the bloody Centralia Massacre in 1864.

Jesse angrily accused the Fords of knowing about Liddil's capture. They lied and told him they didn't know anything. Now they were nervous about the planned robbery set for the next day. Maybe, they thought, the robbery was just an excuse for Jesse to get them alone and kill them as he had killed Ed Miller.

Suddenly, Jesse James reached toward his gun, and the Fords froze. But Jesse simply unbuckled the heavy belt and tossed the guns on a bed. Then he stood on a chair, calmly turned his back on the two brothers, and began dusting the frame around a sign hanging on the wall. At the click of a cocked pistol, Jesse James turned around instinctively, but in that instant, Bob Ford fired from four feet (1.2 meters) away. The gang leader's head flew against the wall from the impact after the bullet struck just above his ear. The most-wanted outlaw in America tumbled dead to the floor.

After the death of Jesse James, Bob Ford was surprised to find himself considered not a hero but a traitor. He and his brother Charlie went on to play themselves in a theatrical production called How I Killed Jesse James *in 1883. But Charlie killed himself the following year. Bob became a policeman and then ran a number of saloons. He was gunned down in his own bar on June 8, 1892.*

Zee and her children, aged 7 and 2, rushed into the room as the Fords rushed out of the house. The Ford brothers telegraphed the shocking news to the sheriff and then surrendered. They were both convicted of murder but were quickly pardoned by the governor. Although Missouri Governor Thomas Crittenden denied that he plotted with the Fords to assassinate Jesse James, he said he was not sorry to see James dead.

The outlaw's body was identified, photographed, and exhibited to hundreds of curious onlookers

Men gathered around the body of outlaw Jesse James as he lay in his coffin.

at the local hotel. Then it was packed in ice and sent to Kearney where hundreds more attended a funeral. Jesse James was laid to rest beneath a coffee bean tree at the Samuel family's farm. Years later, his body was moved to a nearby cemetery. But the legend of Jesse James, one part fact and two parts fiction, refused to lie still. ❧

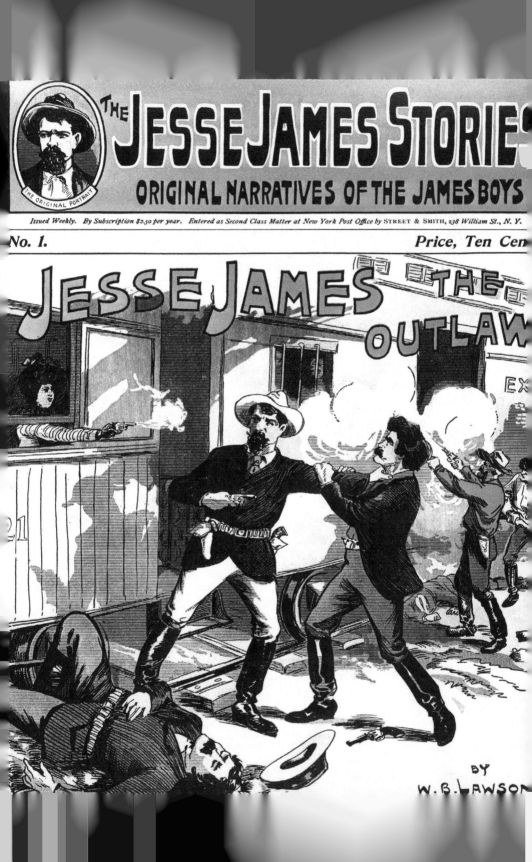

Chapter
10 THE IMAGINARY HERO

⤞⚬⤝

The public fascination with the life of Jesse James only increased after his dramatic death. The more newspapers revealed about his mysterious life, the more people wanted to know. Souvenir hunters immediately began stealing items from the rented house in St. Joseph where Jesse had lived, even peeling off splinters of the fence and barn. Within a week of James' death, the owner of the house was charging visitors 10 cents to see the murder site.

A song appeared about the "dirty little coward that shot Mr. Howard." The ballad spread the idea, created by writer John Newman Edwards, that Jesse James gave his wealth to the poor, and "he'd never see a man suffer pain." Although nothing could have been further from the truth, there was no stopping the legend.

By shooting Jesse James in the head in his own home, Bob Ford turned a dangerous criminal into a tragic victim. The public quickly forgot how James had shot train conductor William Westfall, bank owner John W. Sheets, cashier Joseph Lee Heywood, and many others. But headlines focused on the outlaw's orphaned children and his grief-stricken widow and mother. Zee was left so poor that she was forced to sell off many of her husband's items at auction. She even had to sell Jesse Junior's dog to make ends meet. Within a few months of the funeral, even Jesse's mother was charging a fee to visitors who wanted to see her son's grave.

The first book to include the "true" story of the outlaw's death was rushed into print just seven days after the murder. A stage play about the life of Frank and Jesse opened in a New York theater the same month. The most important early biography appeared seven weeks later. This book, *The Life, Times, and Treacherous Death of Jesse James*, by Frank Triplett, was considered to be true and authentic. Triplett claimed that both Jesse's wife and mother had given him information for the book. Zee, however, told the newspapers, "I know absolutely nothing concerning any and all crimes charged … to my husband."

Biographer Triplett, like John Newman Edwards, took the position that Jesse James was a "good boy gone bad." Jesse James was innocent of his crimes,

James' mother, Zerelda, stood in front of her son's grave in Kearney, Missouri.

the authors said, because the Union Army, the law, the railroads, the Pinkertons, the politicians, and others had left him no choice but the criminal life. Although Jesse James was never a member of the

Confederate Army, he came to symbolize the fighting spirit of the South.

Like his brother, Frank James was never caught or convicted of the many crimes historians believe he committed. In October 1882, with the help of his biographer, John Newman Edwards, Frank James turned himself in to Missouri Governor Crittenden. Frank was treated more like a celebrity than a criminal. He was eventually found innocent of all charges in a series of trials that lasted until 1885. As a free man, Frank worked in a shoe store, a dry goods store, on a farm, and as the doorman at a theater. He even worked as an actor on stage and dreamed of going into politics.

But though he had given up his old ways for good, Frank did ride with the old outlaw gang one more time. In 1903, on the eve of his 60th birthday, he reluctantly joined his friend Cole Younger in a traveling carnival. Younger had been released after 25 years in prison and hoped to make some fast money by telling his story to a new generation. Their show, *The Great Cole Younger and*

Later in life, Frank James reflected on his time as an outlaw and on the influence his example would have on young people. He disagreed with those who called him and his brother heroes. Presenting bad men as heroes in books and plays, Frank said, was harmful to the minds of young boys. Frank strongly objected to a popular play in 1902 called The James Boys of Missouri. "It's injurious to the youth of the country," Frank told The Kansas City Star. "What will the effect [be] on these young men to see train robbers and outlaws glorified?"

Frank James Historical Wild West, lasted less than a year. After his mother died at age 86, Frank returned to the family farm in Kearney, Missouri, where he talked to tourists who paid him 50 cents each. He died in 1915.

Although Jesse died too soon, Frank lived long enough to see an amazing new technology called moving pictures. Movies would spread their story to countless millions of people around the world over the next century. One of the first full-length feature films ever made was called *The Great Train Robbery.* The silent movie appeared in 1903. It was not about the James gang, but it demonstrated the American fascination with crime and violence that contin-

Frank James charged visitors admission to see the family farm in Kearney, Missouri.

ues to this day. The first film officially dedicated to Jesse and Frank James appeared in 1908. Since then, nearly 50 movies about the James brothers have followed. One of these, a 1921 silent film titled *Jesse James Under the Black Flag*, starred Jesse James Jr. in the role of his father. Most of these films cling to the legends started by John Newman Edwards and the early dime novel writers. They are films about an imaginary hero, not a historical criminal.

Falsehoods surround Jesse James' death as well as his life. From the first news of his shooting, there were reports that the man Bob Ford killed was not actually Jesse James. According to rumor, Jesse

Jesse James was the subject of many theatrical productions, fueling a legend that has little connection to the truth.

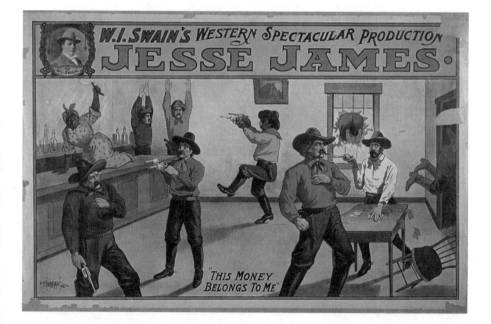

faked his death in order to escape. But the body was clearly identified by those who knew him at the time. It carried the precise scars from bullet wounds and was missing the tip of the left index finger. Still, over the years, a number of people claimed to be the real outlaw.

In 1995, to end the controversy, scientists exhumed the body buried in the family plot in Clay County, Missouri. DNA tests on the remains proved with 99.7 percent accuracy that the body in the grave was, in fact, Jesse Woodson James. The tie tack that James was wearing the day he died was discovered among the remains. So was a bullet, the one that most likely entered the chest of a young bushwhacker during the Civil War and hovered near his heart for 20 years before it was uncovered 113 years later.

There is no longer any dispute: The real Jesse James is dead and buried. But it is safe to say that the make-believe outlaw will live on, far beyond the reach of bullets—and the truth.

JAMES' LIFE

1847

Born in Kearney,
Missouri, September 5

1850

Father leaves to
be a missionary in
California and dies
several months later

1861

Civil War begins;
brother Frank fights
the Union as a mem-
ber of Missouri's
Home Guard

1850

1848

*The Communist
Manifesto* by German
writer Karl Marx is
widely distributed

1860

Postage stamps are
widely used through-
out the world

WORLD EVENTS

1864

Joins Missouri
guerrillas at age 16;
takes part in bloody
Centralia Massacre
on September 27

1865

Civil War ends

1866

Associated with
February 13
bank robbery in
Liberty, Missouri

1865

1863

Construction begins
on the first trans-
continental railroad
in Sacramento,
California

1865

Lewis Carroll
publishes *Alice's
Adventures in
Wonderland*

1867

Russia sells Alaska
to the United States

James' Life

1869

Robs bank in
Gallatin, Missouri,
on December 7

1871

Robs bank in
Corydon, Iowa,
on June 3; hunted
by Pinkertons

1872

Accused of robbing
the Kansas City Fair
on September 26

1870

1869

The periodic table
of elements is
invented by Dimitri
Mendeleyev

1871

P.T. Barnum opens
his traveling circus,
"the greatest show
on Earth"

World Events

1873

Robs train in Adair,
Iowa, on July 21

1874

Robs train in Gads
Hill, Missouri, on
January 31; marries
cousin Zee Mimms on
April 24

1873

Ivy League schools
draw up the first rules
for American football

1874

The first American
zoo is established
in Philadelphia

JAMES' LIFE

1875

Half brother Archie is killed in Pinkerton raid on the Samuel farm; son Jesse is born

1876

Robs train in Rocky Cut, Missouri, on July 6; escapes capture, with brother Frank, after failed bank robbery in Northfield, Minnesota, on September 7

1875

1875

Russian novelist Leo Tolstoy's second masterpiece, *Anna Karenina*, is published in installments, ending in 1877; his epic, *War and Peace*, was published in 1869

1876

Alexander Graham Bell makes the first successful telephone transmission

1877

German inventor Nikolaus A. Otto works on what will become the internal combustion engine for automobiles

WORLD EVENTS

1881

Robs trains in Winston, Missouri, on July 15, and Blue Cut, Missouri, on September 7; governor sets $10,000 reward each for Jesse and Frank

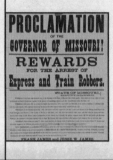

1882

Killed at his home in St. Joseph, Missouri, on April 3 by gang member Bob Ford

1879

Robs Glendale, Missouri, train on October 8; daughter Mary is born

1880

1879

Thomas Edison invents electric lights

1881

Clara Barton founds the Red Cross

DATE OF BIRTH: September 5, 1847

PLACE OF BIRTH: Kearney, Missouri

FATHER: The Reverend Robert James (1818–1850)

MOTHER: Zerelda Cole James Samuel (1825–1911)

EDUCATION: Probably no more than an elementary education

SPOUSE: Zerelda "Zee" Mimms James (1845–1900)

DATE OF MARRIAGE: April 24, 1874

CHILDREN: Jesse (1875–1951)
Gould and Montgomery (twins) (1878)
Mary (1879–1935)

DATE OF DEATH: April 3, 1882

PLACE OF BURIAL: Mount Olivet Cemetery, Kearney, Missouri

FURTHER READING

Bruns, Roger. *Jesse James: Legendary Outlaw.* Springfield, N.J.: Enslow Publishers, 1998.

Hall, Margaret C. *History and Activities of the Civil War.* Chicago: Heinemann Library, 2006.

Saffer, Barbara. *Jesse James.* Philadelphia: Chelsea House Publishers, 2002.

Stiles, T.J. *Jesse James.* Philadelphia: Chelsea House Publishers, 1994.

LOOK FOR MORE SIGNATURE LIVES
BOOKS ABOUT THIS ERA:

James Beckwourth: *Mountaineer, Scout, and Pioneer*
ISBN 0-7565-1000-7

Jim Bridger: *Trapper, Trader, and Guide*
ISBN 0-7565-1870-9

Crazy Horse: *Sioux Warrior*
ISBN 0-7565-0999-8

Geronimo: *Apache Warrior*
ISBN 0-7565-1002-3

Sam Houston: *Texas Hero*
ISBN 0-7565-1004-X

Bridget "Biddy" Mason: *From Slave to Businesswoman*
ISBN 0-7565-1001-5

Zebulon Pike: *Explorer and Soldier*
ISBN 0-7565-0998-X

Sarah Winnemucca: *Scout, Activist, and Teacher*
ISBN 0-7565-1003-1

On the Web

For more information on *Jesse James*, use FactHound.

1. Go to *www.facthound.com*
2. Type in this book ID: 0756518717
3. Click on the *Fetch It* button.

FactHound will find the best Web sites for you.

Historic Sites

The James Farm
21216 Jesse James Farm Road
Kearney, MO 64060
816/628-6065
Birthplace of Jesse James and home base for most of his life

Northfield Historical Society
408 Division St.
Northfield, MN 55057
507/645-9268
Fully restored site of the failed bank robbery on September 7, 1876

abolitionist
a person who supported the banning of slavery

amnesty
an act in which a government grants a pardon for crimes to a group of individuals

bushwhacker
a guerrilla sympathetic to the Confederate cause during the American Civil War

exhume
to dig up something, especially a body, for reburial or for medical investigation

guerrilla
a soldier who is not part of a country's regular army and who fights using small, surprise attacks rather than large battles

irregular
not part of a permanent, organized military force

jayhawker
a Union guerrilla in Kansas and Missouri during the border disputes of 1854–1859

martial law
control of a people by the government's military instead of by civilian forces, often in an emergency

popular sovereignty
the concept that political and legislative power resides with the citizens

vigilantes
people who take the law into their own hands

Chapter 2

Page 20, line 23: T.J. Stiles. *Jesse James: Last Rebel of the Civil War.* New York: A.A. Knopf, 2002, p. 27.

Page 23, line 14: William A. Settle. *Jesse James Was His Name: Or, Fact and Fiction Concerning the Career of the Notorious James Brothers of Missouri.* Lincoln: University of Nebraska, 1977, p. 8.

Page 24, line 10: *Jesse James: Last Rebel of the Civil War*, p. 30.

Page 24, line 23: Ibid., p. 31.

Chapter 3

Page 31, line 2: *Jesse James Was His Name: Or, Fact and Fiction Concerning the Career of the Notorious James Brothers of Missouri*, p. 13.

Page 32, line 26: "Day of Infamy (Part 1)." *Civil War Talk*. 30 March 2005. 26 April 2006. http://civilwartalk.com/forums/printthread.php?t=22023

Page 34, sidebar: *Jesse James: Last Rebel of the Civil War*, p. 91.

Page 36, line 4: *Jesse James Was His Name: Or, Fact and Fiction Concerning the Career of the Notorious James Brothers of Missouri*, p. 27.

Page 36, line 19: Ted P. Yeatman. *Frank and Jesse James: The Story Behind the Legend.* Nashville, Tenn.: Cumberland House, 2000, p. 53.

Chapter 4

Page 43, line 15: Ibid., p. 76.

Chapter 5

Page 47, line 12: *Jesse James Was His Name: Or, Fact and Fiction Concerning the Career of the Notorious James Brothers of Missouri*, p. 33.

Page 50, line 19: *Frank and Jesse James: The Story Behind the Legend*, p. 95.

Page 55, line 5: Ibid., p. 100.

Page 55, line 18: Ibid., p. 103.

Page 55, line 22: *Jesse James Was His Name: Or, Fact and Fiction Concerning the Career of the Notorious James Brothers of Missouri*, p. 45.

Chapter 6

Page 57, line 13: Ibid.

Page 57, line 15: Ibid.

Page 59, line 14: Ibid., p. 105.

Page 59, line 20: Ibid.

Chapter 7

Page 65, line 3: *Frank and Jesse James: The Story Behind the Legend*, p. 137.

Page 66, line 27: Ibid., p. 363.

Page 67, line 9: *Jesse James Was His Name: Or, Fact and Fiction Concerning the Career of the Notorious James Brothers of Missouri*, p. 86.

Page 68, line 6: Robert Dyer. *Jesse James and the Civil War in Missouri.* Columbia: University of Missouri Press, 1994, p. 57.

Chapter 8

Page 71, line 7: John J. Koblas. *Faithful Unto Death.* Northfield, Minn.: Northfield Historical Society Press, 2001, p. 14.

Page 74, line 4: George Huntington. *Robber and Hero: The Story of the Northfield Bank Raid.* Northfield, Minn.: Northfield Historical Society Press, 1994, p. 15.

Page 75, line 11: Ibid., p. 24.

Page 77, line 7: *Jesse James: Last Rebel of the Civil War*, p. 345.

Chapter 9

Page 83, line 4: Marley Brant. *Jesse James: The Man and the Myth.* New York: Berkley Books, 1998 p. 211.

Page 84, line 20: Frank Triplett. *The Life, Times, and Treacherous Death of Jesse James.* Chicago: Swallow Press, 1970, p. 224.

Page 84, line 22: Ibid.

Chapter 10

Page 89, line 10: *Jesse James Was His Name: Or, Fact and Fiction Concerning the Career of the Notorious James Brothers of Missouri*, p. 173.

Page 89, line 13: Ibid.

Page 90, line 24: *The Life, Times, and Treacherous Death of Jesse James*, p. xii.

Page 92, sidebar: *Frank and Jesse James: The Story Behind the Legend*, p. 300.

Brant, Marley. *Jesse James: The Man and the Myth.* New York: Berkley Books, 1998.

Brant, Marley. *Outlaws: The Illustrated History of the James–Younger Gang.* Montgomery, Ala.: Elliott & Clark Pub., 1997.

Dalton, Brad. *The True Story of Jesse James.* San Jose, Calif.: Writers Club Press, 2001.

Dyer, Robert. *Jesse James and the Civil War in Missouri.* Columbia: University of Missouri Press, 1994.

Huntington, George. *Robber and Hero: The Story of the Northfield Bank Raid.* Northfield, Minn.: Northfield Historical Society Press, 1994.

American Experience: Jesse James. Dir. Mark Zwonitzer. PBS. WGBH, Boston. 6 Feb. 2006.

Koblas, John J. *Faithful Unto Death.* Northfield, Minn.: Northfield Historical Society Press, 2001.

Settle, William A. *Jesse James Was His Name: Or, Fact and Fiction Concerning the Careers of the Notorious James Brothers of Missouri.* Lincoln: University of Nebraska Press, 1977.

Starrs, James E. *A Voice for the Dead: A Forensic Investigator's Pursuit of the Truth in the Grave.* New York: Putnam, 2005.

Stiles, T.J. *Jesse James: Last Rebel of the Civil War.* New York: A.A Knopf, 2002.

Triplett, Frank. *The Life, Times, and Treacherous Death of Jesse James.* Chicago: Swallow Press, 1970.

Yeatman, Ted P. *Frank and Jesse James: The Story Behind the Legend.* Nashville, Tenn.: Cumberland House, 2000.

Younger, Cole. *The Story of Cole Younger by Himself: Being an Autobiography of the Missouri Guerrilla Captain and Outlaw, His Capture and Prison Life, and the Only Authentic Account of the Northfield Raid Ever Published.* St. Paul, Minn.: Minnesota Historical Society Press, 2000.

J. Dennis Robinson is editor and owner of the popular New England Web site *SeacoastNH.com*. A lecturer, freelance journalist, and media scriptwriter, he is the author of a number of books about history, including the Signature Lives biography of Lord Baltimore. He lives near the Piscataqua River in Portsmouth, New Hampshire, with his wife, Maryellen.

Image Credits